I0803353

NATIVE AMERICAN NATIONS

Ute

F.A. BIRD

Checkerboard Library

An Imprint of Abdo Publishing

abdobooks.com

ABDOBOOKS.COM
Published by Abdo Publishing, a division of ABDO, PO Box 398166, Minneapolis, Minnesota 55439.
Copyright © 2025 by Abdo Consulting Group, Inc. International copyrights reserved in all countries. No part of this book may be reproduced in any form without written permission from the publisher. Checkerboard Library™ is a trademark and logo of Abdo Publishing.

Printed in the United States of America, North Mankato, Minnesota
102024
012025

THIS BOOK CONTAINS RECYCLED MATERIALS

Editor: Lauri Nelson
Design: Mighty Media, Inc.

Cover Photograph: AP Photo/Rick Bowmer
Interior Photographs: Ad_hominem/Shutterstock Images, p. 7; Angel Wynn/NativeStock, p. 9, 19, 25, 29; Danita Delimont Photography/Newscom, p. 15; Detroit Photographic Co., Publisher. Utes. Jose Romero and family, 1899. [Detroit, Michigan: Detroit Photographic Co] Photograph. https://www.loc.gov/item/2017657483/. , p. 13; Eric Selchert Photography/Shutterstock Images, p. 11; National Museum of the American Indian, Smithsonian Institution (19/7329). Photo by NMAI Photo Services, p. 23; National Museum of the American Indian, Smithsonian Institution (25/3032). Photo by NMAI Photo Services, p. 21; Oscity/Shuttterstock Images, p. 5; Utes--Chief Sevara i.e., Severo and family, ca. 1899. Photograph. https://www.loc.gov/item/96501843/.h, p. 17; W.H. Jackson/The New York Historical Society/Getty Images, p. 27

Library of Congress Control Number: 2024938873

Publisher's Cataloging-in-Publication Data
Names: Bird, F.A., author.
Title: Ute / by F.A. Bird
Description: Minneapolis, Minnesota : ABDO Publishing, 2025 | Series: Native American nations | Includes online resources and index.
Identifiers: ISBN 9781098296278 (lib. bdg.) | ISBN 9798384917380 (ebook)
Subjects: LCSH: Ute Indians--Juvenile literature. | Nūche Indians--Juvenile literature. | Native Americans --Juvenile literature. | Indians of North America--Juvenile literature. | Indigenous peoples--Social life and customs--Juvenile literature. | Cultural anthropology--Juvenile literature.
Classification: DDC 973.0497--dc23

Contents

CHAPTER I

Homelands

The traditional Ute (YOOT) homelands were around the region of the Great Basin and the Colorado Plateau. Their territory included portions of present-day Colorado, Utah, northern New Mexico, and northeastern Arizona.

Centuries of **eroding** winds and rushing rivers carved a beautiful landscape. There were deserts, mountains, plateaus, and canyons. There were also meadows, marshes, and grasslands. The land held forests of ponderosa and lodgepole pine, piñon, juniper, and spruce trees. Dogwood, cottonwood, mesquite, and sagebrush grew at lower levels.

The Ute call themselves the Nuciu (NOO-chee-oh). Nuciu means “the people,” or “high land people.” The Ute spoke Shoshone, which belongs to the Numic branch of the Uto-Aztecan language family. The Ute’s neighbors included the Arapaho, Comanche, Navajo, Paiute, and Shoshone tribes.

Chimney Rock National Monument in Colorado is sacred to the Southern Ute Indian Tribe.

CHAPTER 2

Society

The Ute society was divided into bands. These bands lived in different areas of Ute territory. The bands included the Mouache, Capote, Weeminuche, Tabequache, Grand River, White River, and the Uintah.

The people of each band chose a chief. The chief led by earning the respect of his people. These band chiefs led the people in peace and war. Medicine people also cared for the band members. These people were skilled in using plants and ceremonies to heal.

In the spring, the Ute bands broke into smaller family units. This was necessary for the Ute to survive. The smaller units made traveling easier, which in turn made finding food easier. They followed **migrating** animals and gathered wild berries and vegetables as they ripened.

In winter, the Ute came together again. They socialized and participated in large festivals. Winter was also the time for arranging marriages and holding reunions.

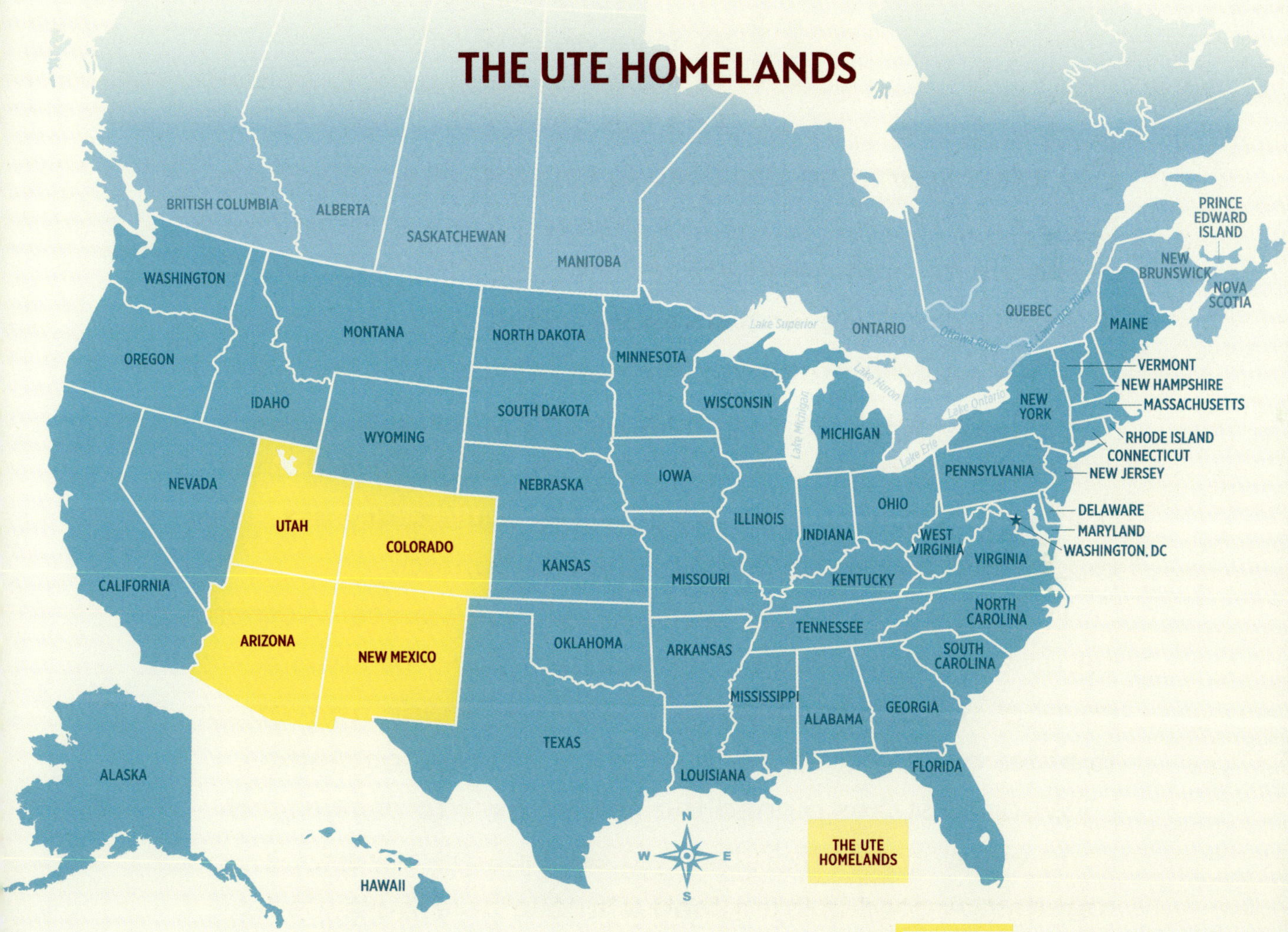

THE UTE HOMELANDS
BRITISH COLUMBIA
ALBERTA
SASKATCHEWAN
MANITOBA
ONTARIO
QUEBEC
PRINCE EDWARD ISLAND
NEW BRUNSWICK
NOVA SCOTIA
Lake Superior
Lake Michigan
Lake Huron
Lake Ontario
Lake Erie
Ottawa River
St. Lawrence River
WASHINGTON
OREGON
IDAHO
MONTANA
NORTH DAKOTA
SOUTH DAKOTA
MINNESOTA
WISCONSIN
MICHIGAN
WYOMING
NEVADA
UTAH
COLORADO
NEBRASKA
IOWA
ILLINOIS
INDIANA
OHIO
PENNSYLVANIA
NEW YORK
MAINE
VERMONT
NEW HAMPSHIRE
MASSACHUSETTS
RHODE ISLAND
CONNECTICUT
NEW JERSEY
DELAWARE
MARYLAND
WASHINGTON, DC
WEST VIRGINIA
VIRGINIA
KENTUCKY
CALIFORNIA
KANSAS
MISSOURI
TENNESSEE
NORTH CAROLINA
SOUTH CAROLINA
ARIZONA
NEW MEXICO
OKLAHOMA
ARKANSAS
MISSISSIPPI
ALABAMA
GEORGIA
TEXAS
LOUISIANA
FLORIDA
ALASKA
HAWAII
N
W
E
S
THE UTE HOMELANDS

CHAPTER 3

Homes

For many years, the Ute lived in brush shelters. Each one held about 12 people. The Ute covered the frames of these shelters with brush. Sometimes they used handwoven reed or grass mats to cover the shelters. They tied these mats onto the wooden frame with willow strips.

The Ute began living in tepees after they were introduced to horses. Tepees were easier to move than brush shelters. That's because horses could carry the tepees from camp to camp as the Ute hunted.

The Ute made tepees with long wooden poles. Women set up the poles to form a cone. Then they stretched a cover over the frame. A tepee cover was made from about 15 **hides** of American bison, or buffalo, sewn together.

Wooden stakes pinned the tepee cover to the ground. Long wooden pins held the two ends of the cover together. A door opening and a smoke hole were made. Inside, the Ute slept on reed mats and furs around a fire.

Two Ute tepees and a wickiup. The brush shelters of the Ute were called wickiups.

CHAPTER 4

Food

Ute men went hunting to find food. They used spears, bows and arrows, and traps. The men hunted large animals, such as elk, bison, and deer. They hunted smaller animals, such as squirrels and rabbits. In addition, the men hunted birds, such as ducks, quail, doves, and grouse.

The Ute fished using a hook and line. They also used wooden spears. The spears had barbs, or sharp points, at the end. These barbs prevented the fish from flopping off the spear. The Ute fished for trout, bass, and other panfish.

The Ute also gathered barks, roots, wild vegetables, and medicinal plants. When the Ute planted gardens, they grew corn, beans, and squash. They ground the corn into flour and used it to make bread and mush.

The Ute ate their food in season. But they also saved some food for the winter by drying their meat and fish. They mixed the dried meats with wild berries and buffalo fat to make pemmican (PEM-ih-ken).

Elk are one of the largest members of the deer family. Large males are called bulls. Only male elk have antlers.

CHAPTER 5

Clothing

The Ute made and decorated their clothing with the materials and animals they found in their environment. What they did not eat, they used for clothing, decoration, or tools. There was no waste.

The Ute made their clothing from deer, elk, and buffalo skins. They sewed with thread made from animal **sinew**. Needles were carved from bone. They used sharp antlers, bones, and stones to punch holes in **hides**.

Men wore fringed leather shirts, **breechcloths**, leggings, and moccasins. The leggings had long fringes along the outside seam. Sometimes, the Ute painted or quilled the fringes that were on their shirts and leggings.

Women wore long, fringed leather dresses. The dresses were decorated with elk teeth, bear claws, or shells. Ute women wore wide belts. They also wore fringed leggings under their dresses. They wrapped the legging around the leg between the knee and the top of the moccasin.

Later, the Ute also wore items made of cloth. This became available through trade.

CHAPTER 6

Crafts

The Ute were skilled artisans. One skill was making baskets. Women crafted **utility**, medicine, and wedding baskets from reeds and willow. They used natural dyes to color the basket materials red, black, or yellow.

Women decorated clothing with porcupine quills. They dyed some of the porcupine quills for this purpose. Quills were hard when dry. So, women wet the quills to soften them and quickly sewed them onto clothing. They made beautiful **geometric** and floral designs with the quills.

Today, Ute women commonly use glass beads instead of quills. Glass beads were introduced by European traders. The Ute decorate **cradleboard** covers, vests, leggings, moccasins, rattle handles, and more with beads.

Women use two types of beading stitches. The peyote stitch is used on rattle handles. The lazy stitch is used for beading on clothing. The lazy stitch can be used to bead floral, geometric, and animal designs.

Coin purse decorated with Ute beadwork

CHAPTER 7

Family

Ute families were close. An extended family of aunts, uncles, cousins, and grandparents lived together in a camp. Every family member was important to the survival of the band. Each person contributed to the daily chores.

Men hunted for food and protected the families. They made the tools and weapons they needed for hunting and fishing. They made these tools from bone, flint, and antler. Men also made knives and stone axes. They used the axes to harvest trees they would later use for their tepees.

Women were responsible for the home, food, and clothing. They used digging sticks to harvest wild onions and other roots that were safe to eat. Women gathered berries and medicinal plants in woven baskets. They were also responsible for drying food for the winter.

The elders of the band showed young ones how to weave and make tools and weapons. They also told the history of the Ute and taught the children by telling stories.

Ute Chief Severo *(top left)* and his family.

CHAPTER 8

Children

The Ute loved their children and taught them important skills. Children learned by watching and helping with daily chores. Girls watched as older women made **cradleboards**.

A cradleboard was made from willow. At the top, a willow band kept the baby's head safe. The baby was placed inside a leather pouch that covered the board. An older girl might carry a baby in a cradleboard on her back.

Ute boys learned from watching the men in their band. Boys learned to hunt and fish. They hunted rabbits and other small game with bows and arrows. Older boys learned to identify animal tracks and quietly follow them.

However, the children did not spend all their time watching the adults. They also played games. One game was played with a **vertebra** of a bird. The children attached a short cord to the vertebra. At the other end of the cord was a small wooden pin. The object of the game was to catch the vertebra on the wooden pin.

A cradleboard's oval frame was wide at the top, and it narrowed toward the bottom.

CHAPTER 9

Traditions

In the winter, the Ute told stories around their campfires. One of these stories recounts how the earth was created.

A long time ago, the world we know today did not exist. In the Sky World, the Creator sat alone. He opened a hole in the Sky World, picked up a giant broom, and began to sweep pebbles, dust, and dirt through the hole. The Creator looked down and was delighted that the dust, dirt, and pebbles became mountains, plateaus, and rolling hills.

The Creator poured water and ice through the Sky Hole. This became rain and snow. They made everything look pretty. In the moist soil, the Creator planted trees, flowers, and other plants.

The Creator picked up fallen leaves and threw them into the air. The leaves became birds with beautiful songs and colors. Then, he created the Ute. He created animals and fish. He taught the Ute how to do ceremonies and how to hunt and fish.

"Ute Culture" by Russell Box Senior, a Southern Ute elder, shows the Creator pouring water through the Sky Hole.

CHAPTER 10

War

Before meeting Europeans, war was rare among the Ute. But, sometimes the Ute fought when neighboring tribes invaded their lands. These wars were necessary to protect Ute hunting, fishing, and gathering territory.

In war, the Ute used bows and arrows for distant fighting. In close fighting, they used knives with blades made of quartz, a clear, hard mineral. The Ute often painted their faces and clothes before going into battle.

The Ute wore breastplates made from bone beads. They also wore wide bone-bead chokers around their necks. Breastplates and chokers were worn like armor. The bone beads protected the wearer's neck and chest from arrows.

Sometimes the Ute did not kill the enemy. Instead they counted coup. This meant riding into the enemy's camp and touching the enemy with a stick. This was a great show of bravery for the Ute, and no one died.

Rawhide war shield with painted cover. A war shield gave both physical and spiritual protection, and it showed the cultural identity of the man who used it.

CHAPTER II

Contact with Europeans

In the 1600s, the Ute traded with Spaniards who lived in what is now New Mexico. The Ute became one of the first native peoples to have horses because of this trade.

However, not all contact with Europeans was positive. Around the 1850s, miners found gold and copper in Ute territory. Settlers flooded into the area hoping to get rich. They wanted the Ute's lands. The Ute fought back.

The Ute also had no **immunity** to European illnesses. Many died from **measles epidemics**. Soon, the Ute were forced to sign treaties and give up large areas of land. They were relocated to reservations.

Once on reservations, the US government wanted the Ute people to give up some of their ways. It wanted them to settle in one place and be farmers. The US government even outlawed Ute ceremonies such as the sun dance.

American traders and Southern Ute at the Abiquiu Indian Agency, New Mexico, in 1870.

CHAPTER 12

Ouray

Ouray (OO-ray) was a famous Ute chief. He was born in 1833. Ouray grew up in a time of great conflict for the Ute. Both settlers and the US government wanted Ute lands. The Ute had to fight to protect their lands and way of life.

Ouray saw the war and bloodshed. He saw how neighboring tribes were being mistreated. Ouray did not want his people to suffer.

Ouray believed the best way to prevent bloodshed was to arrange treaties with the US government. Because he spoke several languages, including English, it was easier for him to arrange these peace treaties. Ouray even met with President Ulysses Grant to protect the Ute people.

Ouray did what he could to protect his people and his land. He tried his best to negotiate respectfully with the new settlers. However, the Ute were eventually confined to a reservation set aside for them by the US government. Ouray died in 1880.

Chief Ouray

CHAPTER 13

The Ute Today

Today, the Ute live on three federally recognized reservations. One is the Uintah and Ouray Reservation, located in Utah. Another is the Southern Ute Reservation, located near Ignacio, Colorado. The third is called the Ute Mountain Reservation near Towaoc, Colorado.

The Ute **economy** has changed much in the Ute's long history. Today, much of their income is earned from the sale of natural resources such as timber, gas, and oil. One of the Ute reservations even has a pottery plant.

The Ute are working to preserve their culture. Annual dances such as the bear and sun dance are the foundation of Ute traditions. Sun dances are sacred and held in the summer. The bear dance is held in springtime. During the dance there is also singing, eating, and prayer offerings.

The Ute continue to make their traditional crafts. They bead purses, vests, ties, moccasins, and other clothing as they preserve their traditional skills through art.

Miss Ute Tribe at a parade on the Uintah and Ouray Reservation in Fort Duchesne, Utah.

Glossary

artisan—a person skilled in a craft or trade.

breechcloth—a piece of hide or cloth, usually worn by men, that is wrapped between the legs and tied with a belt around the waist.

cradleboard—a flat board used to hold a baby. It could be carried on the mother's back or hung from a tree so that the baby could see what was going on.

economy—the way a tribe uses its money, goods, and natural resources.

epidemic—the rapid spread of a disease among many people.

erode—to wash or wear away.

federal recognition—the US government's recognition of a tribe as being an independent nation. The tribe is eligible for special funding and protection of its lands.

geometric—made up of straight lines, circles, and other simple shapes.

hide—an animal skin that is often thick and heavy.

immunity—protection against disease.

measles—an illness that causes a fever and rash.

migrate—to move from one place to another.

sinew—a band of tough fibers that joins a muscle to a bone.

utility—made to be used in a practical way.

vertebra—one of the bones that makes up the backbone.

ONLINE RESOURCES

Booklinks
NONFICTION NETWORK
FREE! ONLINE NONFICTION RESOURCES

To learn more about the Ute, please visit **abdobooklinks.com** or scan this QR code. These links are routinely monitored and updated to provide the most current information available.

Index